The Constitution of
The State of Minnesota:
A Quick Reference Guide

Bootblack Budget Books
Copyright 2018 ©
ISBN-13: 978-1986792240
ISBN-10: 1986792242

Contents:

Preamble – Page 18

Article I: Bill of Rights – Page 19

Section 1. Object of government.

Section 2. Rights and privileges.

Section 3. Liberty of the press.

Section 4. Trial by jury.

Section 5. No excessive bail or unusual punishments.

Section 7. Due process; prosecutions; double jeopardy; self-incrimination; bail; habeas corpus.

Section 8. Redress of injuries or wrongs.

Section 9. Treason defined.

Section 10. Unreasonable searches and seizures prohibited.

Section 11. Attainders, ex post facto laws and laws impairing contracts prohibited.

Section 12. Imprisonment for debt; property exemption.

Section 13. Private property for public use.

Section 14. Military power subordinate.

Section 15. Lands allodial; void agricultural leases.

Section 16. Freedom of conscience; no preference to be given to any religious establishment or mode of worship.

Section 17. Religious tests and property qualifications prohibited.

Article II: Name and Boundaries – Page 25

Section 1. Name and boundaries; acceptance of organic act.

Section 2. Jurisdiction on boundary waters.

Article III: Distribution of the Powers of Government – Page 26

Section 1. Division of powers.

Article IV: Legislative Department – Page 27

Section 1. Composition of legislature.

Section 2. Apportionment of members.

Section 3. Census enumeration apportionment; congressional and legislative district boundaries; senate districts.

Section 4. Terms of office of senators and representatives; vacancies.

Section 5. Restriction on holding office.

Section 6. Qualification of legislators; judging election returns and eligibility.

Section 7. Rules of government.

Section 8. Oath of office.

Section 9. Compensation.

Section 10. Privilege from arrest.

Section 11. Protest and dissent of members.

Section 12. Biennial meetings; length of session; special sessions; length of adjournments.

Section 13. Quorum.

Section 14. Open sessions.

Section 15. Officers; journals.

Section 16. Elections viva voce.

Section 17. Laws to embrace only one subject.

Section 18. Revenue bills to originate in house.

Section 19. Reporting of bills.

Section 20. Enrollment of bills.

Section 21. Passage of bills on last day of session prohibited.

Section 23. Approval of bills by governor; action on veto.

Section 24. Presentation of orders, resolutions, and votes to governor.

Section 25. Disorderly conduct.

Section 26. Banking laws; two-thirds votes.

Article V: Executive Department – Page 36

Section 1. Executive officers.

Section 2. Term of governor and lieutenant governor; qualifications.

Section 3. Powers and duties of governor.

Section 4. Terms and salaries of executive officers.

Section 5. Succession to offices of governor and lieutenant governor.

Section 7. Board of pardons.

Article VI: Judiciary – Page 39

Section 1. Judicial power.

Section 2. Supreme court.

Section 3. Jurisdiction of district court.

Section 4. Judicial districts; district judges.

Section 5. Qualifications; compensation.

Section 6. Holding other office.

Section 7. Term of office; election.

Section 8. Vacancy.

Section 9. Retirement, removal and discipline.

Section 10. Retired judges.

Section 11. Probate jurisdiction.

Section 13. District court clerks.

Article VII: Elective Franchise – Page 43

Section 1. Eligibility; place of voting; ineligible persons.

Section 2. Residence.

Section 3. Uniform oath at elections.

Section 4. Civil process suspended on election day.

Section 5. Elections by ballot.

Section 6. Eligibility to hold office.

Section 7. Official year of state.

Section 8. Election returns to secretary of state; board of canvassers.

Section 9. Campaign spending limits.

Article VIII: Impeachment and Removal from Office – Page 46

Section 1. Impeachment powers.

Section 2. Officers subject to impeachment; grounds; judgment.

Section 3. Suspension.

Section 4. Service of impeachment papers.

Section 5. Removal of inferior officers.

Section 6. Recall.

Article IX: Amendments to the Constitution – Page 49

Section 1. Amendments; ratification.

Section 2. Constitutional convention.

Section 3. Submission to people of constitution drafted at convention.

Article X: Taxation – Page 51

Section 1. Power of taxation; exemptions; legislative powers.

Section 2. Forestation.

Section 3. Occupation tax; ores.

Section 4. Motor fuel taxation.

Section 5. Aircraft.

Section 6. Taconite taxation.

Section 7. Repealed.

Section 8. Parimutuel betting.

Article XI: Appropriations and Finances – Page 54

Section 1. Money paid from state treasury.

Section 2. Credit of the state limited.

Section 3. Internal improvements prohibited; exceptions.

Section 4. Power to contract public debt; public debt defined.

Section 5. Public debt and works of internal improvement; purposes.

Section 6. Certificates of indebtedness.

Section 7. Bonds.

Section 8. Permanent school fund; source; investment; board of investment.

Section 9. Investment of permanent university fund; restrictions.

Section 10. Exchange of public lands; reservation of rights.

Section 11. Timber lands set apart as state forests; disposition of revenue.

Section 12. County, township or municipal aid to railroads limited.

Section 13. Safekeeping state funds; security; deposit of funds; embezzlement.

Section 14. Environment and natural resources fund.

Section 15. Outdoor heritage, clean water, parks and trails, and arts and cultural heritage; sales tax dedicated funds.

Article XII: Special Legislation; Local Government – Page 64

Section 1. Prohibition of special legislation; particular subjects.

Section 2. Special laws; local government.

Section 3. Local government; legislation affecting.

Section 4. Home rule charter.

Section 5. Charter commissions.

Article XIII: Miscellaneous Subjects – Page 67

Section 1. Uniform system of public schools.

Section 2. Prohibition as to aiding sectarian school.

Section 3. University of Minnesota.

Section 4. Lands taken for public way or use; compensation; common carriers.

Section 5. Lotteries.

Section 7. No license required to peddle.

Section 8. Veterans' bonus.

Section 9. Militia organization.

Section 10. Seat of government.

Section 11. State seal.

Section 12. Preservation of hunting and fishing.

Article XIV: Public Highway System – Page 70

Section 1. Authority of state; participation of political subdivisions.

Section 2. Trunk highway system.

Section 3. County state-aid highway system.

Section 4. Municipal state-aid street system.

Section 5. Highway user tax distribution fund.

Section 6. Trunk highway fund.

Section 7. County state-aid highway fund.

Section 8. Municipal state-aid street fund.

Section 9. Taxation of motor vehicles.

Section 10. Taxation of motor fuel.

Section 11. Highway bonds.

Section 12. Motor vehicle sales tax apportionment.

Section 13. Motor vehicle sales tax allocation.

Preamble

We, the people of the state of Minnesota, grateful to God for our civil and religious liberty, and desiring to perpetuate its blessings and secure the same to ourselves and our posterity, do ordain and establish this Constitution

ARTICLE I: BILL OF RIGHTS

Section 1. Object of Government

Government is instituted for the security, benefit and protection of the people, in whom all political power is inherent, together with the right to alter, modify or reform government whenever required by the public good.

Section 2. Rights and Privileges

No member of this state shall be disfranchised or deprived of any of the rights or privileges secured to any citizen thereof, unless by the law of the land or the judgment of his peers. There shall be neither slavery nor involuntary servitude in the state otherwise than as punishment for a crime of which the party has been convicted.

Section 3. Liberty of the Press

The liberty of the press shall forever remain inviolate, and all persons may freely speak, write and publish their sentiments on all subjects, being responsible for the abuse of such right.

Section 4. Trial by Jury

The right of trial by jury shall remain inviolate, and shall extend to all cases at law without regard to the amount in controversy. A jury trial may be waived by the parties in all cases in the manner prescribed by law. The legislature may provide that the agreement of five-sixths of a jury in a civil action or proceeding, after not less than six hours' deliberation, is a sufficient verdict. The legislature may provide for the number of jurors in a civil action or proceeding, provided that a jury have at least six members.

Section 5. No Excessive Bail or Unusual Punishments

Excessive bail shall not be required, nor excessive fines imposed, nor cruel or unusual punishments inflicted.
Section 6. Rights of accused in criminal prosecutions.In all criminal prosecutions the accused shall enjoy the right to a speedy and public trial by an impartial jury of the county or district wherein the crime shall have been committed, which county or district shall have been previously ascertained by law. In all prosecutions of crimes defined by law as felonies, the accused has the right to a jury of 12 members. In all other criminal prosecutions, the legislature may provide for the number of jurors, provided that a jury have at least six members. The accused shall enjoy the right to be informed of the nature and cause of the accusation, to be confronted with the witnesses against him, to have compulsory process for obtaining witnesses in his favor and to have the assistance of counsel in his defense.

Section 7. Due Process; Prosecutions; Double Jeopardy; Self-Incrimination; Bail; Habeas Corpus

No person shall be held to answer for a criminal offense without due process of law, and no person shall be put twice in jeopardy of punishment for the same offense, nor be compelled in any criminal case to be a witness against himself, nor be deprived of life, liberty or property without due process of law. All persons before conviction shall be bailable by sufficient sureties, except for capital offenses when the proof is evident or the presumption great. The privilege of the writ of habeas corpus shall not be suspended unless the public safety requires it in case of rebellion or invasion.

Section 8. Redress of Injuries or Wrongs

Every person is entitled to a certain remedy in the laws for all injuries or wrongs which he may receive to his person, property or character, and to obtain justice freely and without purchase, completely and without denial, promptly and without delay, conformable to the laws.

Section 9. Treason Defined

Treason against the state consists only in levying war against the state, or in adhering to its enemies, giving them aid and comfort. No person shall be convicted of treason unless on the testimony of two witnesses to the same overt act or on confession in open court.

Section 10. Unreasonable Searches and Seizures Prohibited

The right of the people to be secure in their persons, houses, papers, and effects against unreasonable searches and seizures shall not be violated; and no warrant shall issue but upon probable cause, supported by oath or affirmation, and particularly describing the place to be searched and the person or things to be seized.

Section 11. Attainders, Ex Post Facto Laws and Laws Impairing Contracts Prohibited

No bill of attainder, ex post facto law, or any law impairing the obligation of contracts shall be passed, and no conviction shall work corruption of blood or forfeiture of estate.

Section 12. Imprisonment for Debt; Property Exemption

No person shall be imprisoned for debt in this state, but this shall not prevent the legislature from providing for imprisonment, or holding to bail, persons charged with fraud in contracting said debt. A reasonable amount of property shall be exempt from seizure or sale for the payment of any debt or liability. The amount of such exemption shall be determined by law. Provided, however, that all property so exempted shall be liable to seizure and sale for any debts incurred to any person for work done or materials furnished in the construction, repair or improvement of the same, and provided further, that such liability to seizure and sale shall also extend to all real property for any debt to any laborer or servant for labor or service performed.

Section 13. Private Property for Public Use

Private property shall not be taken, destroyed or damaged for public use without just compensation therefor, first paid or secured.

Section 14. Military Power Subordinate

The military shall be subordinate to the civil power and no standing army shall be maintained in this state in times of peace.

Section 15. Lands Allodial; Void Agricultural Leases

All lands within the state are allodial and feudal tenures of every description with all their incidents are prohibited. Leases and grants of agricultural lands for a longer period than 21 years reserving rent or service of any kind shall be void.

Section 16. Freedom of Conscience; No Preference to be Given to Any Religious Establishment or Mode of Worship

The enumeration of rights in this constitution shall not deny or impair others retained by and inherent in the people. The right of every man to worship God according to the dictates of his own conscience shall never be infringed; nor shall any man be compelled to attend, erect or support any place of worship, or to maintain any religious or ecclesiastical ministry, against his consent; nor shall any control of or interference with the rights of conscience be permitted, or any preference be given by law to any religious establishment or mode of worship; but the liberty of conscience hereby secured shall not be so construed as to excuse acts of licentiousness or justify practices inconsistent with the peace or safety of the state, nor shall any money be drawn from the treasury for the benefit of any religious societies or religious or theological seminaries.

Section 17. Religious Tests and Property Qualifications Prohibited

No religious test or amount of property shall be required as a qualification for any office of public trust in the state. No religious test or amount of property shall be required as a qualification of any voter at any election in this state; nor shall any person be rendered incompetent to give evidence in any court of law or equity in consequence of his opinion upon the subject of religion.

ARTICLE II: NAME AND BOUNDARIES

Section 1. Name and Boundaries; Acceptance of Organic Act

This state shall be called the state of Minnesota and shall consist of and have jurisdiction over the territory embraced in the act of Congress entitled, "An act to authorize the people of the Territory of Minnesota to form a constitution and state government, preparatory to their admission into the Union on equal footing with the original states," and the propositions contained in that act are hereby accepted, ratified and confirmed, and remain irrevocable without the consent of the United States.

Section 2. Jurisdiction on Boundary Waters

The state of Minnesota has concurrent jurisdiction on the Mississippi and on all other rivers and waters forming a common boundary with any other state or states. Navigable waters leading into the same, shall be common highways and forever free to citizens of the United States without any tax, duty, impost or toll therefor.

ARTICLE III: DISTRIBUTION OF THE POWERS OF GOVERNMENT

Section 1. Division of Powers.

The powers of government shall be divided into three distinct departments: legislative, executive and judicial. No person or persons belonging to or constituting one of these departments shall exercise any of the powers properly belonging to either of the others except in the instances expressly provided in this constitution.

ARTICLE IV: LEGISLATIVE DEPARTMENT

Section 1. Composition of Legislature

The legislature consists of the senate and house of representatives.

Section 2. Apportionment of Members

The number of members who compose the senate and house of representatives shall be prescribed by law. The representation in both houses shall be apportioned equally throughout the different sections of the state in proportion to the population thereof.

Section 3. Census Enumeration Apportionment; Congressional and Legislative District Boundaries; Senate Districts

At its first session after each enumeration of the inhabitants of this state made by the authority of the United States, the legislature shall have the power to prescribe the bounds of congressional and legislative districts. Senators shall be chosen by single districts of convenient contiguous territory. No representative district shall be divided in the formation of a senate district. The senate districts shall be numbered in a regular series.

Section 4. Terms of Office of Senators and Representatives; Vacancies

Representatives shall be chosen for a term of two years, except to fill a vacancy. Senators shall be chosen for a term of four years, except to fill a vacancy and except there shall be an entire new election of all the senators at the first election of representatives after each new legislative apportionment provided for in this article. The governor shall call elections to fill vacancies in either house of the legislature.

Section 5. Restriction on Holding Office

No senator or representative shall hold any other office under the authority of the United States or the state of Minnesota, except that of postmaster or of notary public. If elected or appointed to another office, a legislator may resign from the legislature by tendering his resignation to the governor.

Section 6. Qualification of Legislators; Judging Election Returns and Eligibility

Senators and representatives shall be qualified voters of the state, and shall have resided one year in the state and six months immediately preceding the election in the district from which elected. Each house shall be the judge of the election returns and eligibility of its own members. The legislature shall prescribe by law the manner for taking evidence in cases of contested seats in either house.

Section 7. Rules of Government

Each house may determine the rules of its proceedings, sit upon its own adjournment, punish its members for disorderly behavior, and with the concurrence of two-thirds expel a member; but no member shall be expelled a second time for the same offense.

Section 8. Oath of Office

Each member and officer of the legislature before entering upon his duties shall take an oath or affirmation to support the Constitution of the United States, the constitution of this state, and to discharge faithfully the duties of his office to the best of his judgment and ability.

Section 9. Compensation

The salary of senators and representatives shall be prescribed by a council consisting of the following members: one person who is not a judge from each congressional district appointed by the chief justice of the Supreme Court, and one member from each congressional district appointed by the governor. If Minnesota has an odd number of congressional districts, the governor and the chief justice must each appoint an at-large member in addition to a member from each congressional district. One-half of the members appointed by the governor and one-half of the members appointed by the chief justice must belong to the political party that has the most members in the legislature. One-half of the members appointed by the governor and one-half of the members appointed by the chief justice must belong to the political party that has the second-most members in the legislature. None of the members of the council may be current or former legislators, or the spouse of a current legislator. None of the members of the council may be current or former lobbyists registered under Minnesota law. None of the members of the council may be a current employee of the legislature. None of the members of the council may be a current or former judge. None of the members of the council may be a current or former governor, lieutenant governor, attorney general, secretary of state, or state auditor. None of the members of the council may be a current employee of an entity in the executive or judicial branch. Membership terms, removal, and compensation of members shall be as provided by law. The council must prescribe salaries by March 31 of each odd-numbered year, taking into account any other legislative compensation provided to legislators by the state of Minnesota, with any changes in salary to take effect on July 1 of that year. Any salary increase for legislators authorized in law by the legislature after January 5, 2015, is repealed.

Section 10. Privilege from Arrest

The members of each house in all cases except treason, felony and breach of the peace, shall be privileged from arrest during the session of their respective houses and in going to or returning from the same. For any speech or debate in either house they shall not be questioned in any other place.

Section 11. Protest and Dissent of Members

Two or more members of either house may dissent and protest against any act or resolution which they think injurious to the public or to any individual and have the reason of their dissent entered in the journal.

Section 12. Biennial Meetings; Length of Session; Special Sessions; Length of Adjournments

The legislature shall meet at the seat of government in regular session in each biennium at the times prescribed by law for not exceeding a total of 120 legislative days. The legislature shall not meet in regular session, nor in any adjournment thereof, after the first Monday following the third Saturday in May of any year. After meeting at a time prescribed by law, the legislature may adjourn to another time. "Legislative day" shall be defined by law. A special session of the legislature may be called by the governor on extraordinary occasions.

Neither house during a session of the legislature shall adjourn for more than three days (Sundays excepted) nor to any other place than that in which the two houses shall be assembled without the consent of the other house.

Section 13. Quorum

A majority of each house constitutes a quorum to transact business, but a smaller number may adjourn from day to day and compel the attendance of absent members in the manner and under the penalties it may provide.

Section 14. Open Sessions

Each house shall be open to the public during its sessions except in cases which in its opinion require secrecy.

Section 15. Officers; Journals

Each house shall elect its presiding officer and other officers as may be provided by law. Both houses shall keep journals of their proceedings, and from time to time publish the same, and the yeas and nays, when taken on any question, shall be entered in the journals.

Section 16. Elections viva voce

In all elections by the legislature members shall vote viva voce and their votes shall be entered in the journal.

Section 17. Laws to Embrace Only One Subject

No law shall embrace more than one subject, which shall be expressed in its title.

Section 18. Revenue Bills to Originate in House

All bills for raising revenue shall originate in the house of representatives, but the senate may propose and concur with the amendments as on other bills.

Section 19. Reporting of Bills

Every bill shall be reported on three different days in each house, unless, in case of urgency, two-thirds of the house where the bill is pending deem it expedient to dispense with this rule.

Section 20. Enrollment of Bills

Every bill passed by both houses shall be enrolled and signed by the presiding officer of each house. Any presiding officer refusing to sign a bill passed by both houses shall thereafter be disqualified from any office of honor or profit in the state. Each house by rule shall provide the manner in which a bill shall be certified for presentation to the governor in case of such refusal.

Section 21. Passage of Bills on Last Day of Session Prohibited

No bill shall be passed by either house upon the day prescribed for adjournment. This section shall not preclude the enrollment of a bill or its transmittal from one house to the other or to the executive for his signature.
Section 22. Majority vote of all members to pass a law. The style of all laws of this state shall be: "Be it enacted by the legislature of the state of Minnesota." No law shall be passed unless voted for by a majority of all the members elected to each house of the legislature, and the vote entered in the journal of each house.

Section 23. Approval of Bills by Governor; Action on Veto

Every bill passed in conformity to the rules of each house and the joint rules of the two houses shall be presented to the governor. If he approves a bill, he shall sign it, deposit it in the office of the secretary of state and notify the house in which it originated of that fact. If he vetoes a bill, he shall return it with his objections to the house in which it originated. His objections shall be entered in the journal. If, after reconsideration, two-thirds of that house agree to pass the bill, it shall be sent, together with the governor's objections, to the other house, which shall likewise reconsider it. If approved by two-thirds of that house it becomes a law and shall be deposited in the office of the secretary of state. In such cases the votes of both houses shall be determined by yeas and nays, and the names of the persons voting for or against the bill shall be entered in the journal of each house. Any bill not returned by the governor within three days (Sundays excepted) after it is presented to him becomes a law as if he had signed it, unless the legislature by adjournment within that time prevents its return. Any bill passed during the last three days of a session may be presented to the governor during the three days following the day of final adjournment and becomes law if the governor signs and deposits it in the office of the secretary of state within 14 days after the adjournment of the legislature. Any bill passed during the last three days of the session which is not signed and deposited within 14 days after adjournment does not become a law.

If a bill presented to the governor contains several items of appropriation of money, he may veto one or more of the items while approving the bill. At the time he signs the bill the governor shall append to it a statement of the items he vetoes and the vetoed items shall not take effect. If the legislature is in session, he shall transmit to the house in which the bill originated a copy of the statement, and the items vetoed shall be separately reconsidered. If on reconsideration any item is approved by two-thirds of the members elected to each house, it is a part of the law notwithstanding the objections of the governor.

Section 24. Presentation of Orders, Resolutions, and Votes to Governor

Each order, resolution or vote requiring the concurrence of the two houses except such as relate to the business or adjournment of the legislature shall be presented to the governor and is subject to his veto as prescribed in case of a bill.

Section 25. Disorderly Conduct

During a session each house may punish by imprisonment for not more than 24 hours any person not a member who is guilty of any disorderly or contemptuous behavior in its presence.

Section 26. Banking Laws; Two-Thirds Votes

Passage of a general banking law requires the vote of two-thirds of the members of each house of the legislature.

ARTICLE V: EXECUTIVE DEPARTMENT

Section 1. Executive Officers

The executive department consists of a governor, lieutenant governor, secretary of state, auditor, and attorney general, who shall be chosen by the electors of the state. The governor and lieutenant governor shall be chosen jointly by a single vote applying to both offices in a manner prescribed by law.

Section 2. Term of Governor and Lieutenant Governor; Qualifications

The term of office for the governor and lieutenant governor is four years and until a successor is chosen and qualified. Each shall have attained the age of 25 years and, shall have been a bona fide resident of the state for one year next preceding his election, and shall be a citizen of the United States.

Section 3. Powers and Duties of Governor

The governor shall communicate by message to each session of the legislature information touching the state and country. He is commander-in-chief of the military and naval forces and may call them out to execute the laws, suppress insurrection and repel invasion. He may require the opinion in writing of the principal officer in each of the executive departments upon any subject relating to his duties. With the advice and consent of the senate he may appoint notaries public and other officers provided by law. He may appoint commissioners to take the acknowledgment of deeds or other instruments in writing to be used in the state. He shall take care that the laws be faithfully executed. He shall fill any vacancy that may occur in the offices of secretary of state, auditor, attorney general and the other state and district offices hereafter created by law until the end of the term for which the person who had vacated the office was elected or the first Monday in January following the next general election, whichever is sooner, and until a successor is chosen and qualified.

Section 4. Terms and Salaries of Executive Officers

The term of office of the secretary of state, attorney general and state auditor is four years and until a successor is chosen and qualified. The duties and salaries of the executive officers shall be prescribed by law.

Section 5. Succession to Offices of Governor and Lieutenant Governor

In case a vacancy occurs from any cause whatever in the office of governor, the lieutenant governor shall be governor during such vacancy. The compensation of the lieutenant governor shall be prescribed by law. The last elected presiding officer of the senate shall become lieutenant governor in case a vacancy occurs in that office. In case the governor is unable to discharge the powers and duties of his office, the same devolves on the lieutenant governor. The legislature may provide by law for the case of the removal, death, resignation, or inability both of the governor and lieutenant governor to discharge the duties of governor and may provide by law for continuity of government in periods of emergency resulting from disasters caused by enemy attack in this state, including but not limited to, succession to the powers and duties of

public office and change of the seat of government.
Section 6. Oath of office of state officers. Each officer created by this article before entering upon his duties shall take an oath or affirmation to support the constitution of the United States and of this state and to discharge faithfully the duties of his office to the best of his judgment and ability.

Section 7. Board of Pardons

The governor, the attorney general and the chief justice of the supreme court constitute a board of pardons. Its powers and duties shall be defined and regulated by law. The governor in conjunction with the board of pardons has power to grant reprieves and pardons after conviction for an offense against the state except in cases of impeachment.

ARTICLE VI: JUDICIARY

Section 1. Judicial Power

The judicial power of the state is vested in a supreme court, a court of appeals, if established by the legislature, a district court and such other courts, judicial officers and commissioners with jurisdiction inferior to the district court as the legislature may establish.

Section 2. Supreme Court

The supreme court consists of one chief judge and not less than six nor more than eight associate judges as the legislature may establish. It shall have original jurisdiction in such remedial cases as are prescribed by law, and appellate jurisdiction in all cases, but there shall be no trial by jury in the supreme court.

The legislature may establish a court of appeals and provide by law for the number of its judges, who shall not be judges of any other court, and its organization and for the review of its decisions by the supreme court. The court of appeals shall have appellate jurisdiction over all courts, except the supreme court, and other appellate jurisdiction as prescribed by law.

As provided by law judges of the court of appeals or of the district court may be assigned temporarily to act as judges of the supreme court upon its request and judges of the district court may be assigned temporarily by the supreme court to act as judges of the court of appeals.
The supreme court shall appoint to serve at its pleasure a clerk, a reporter, a state law librarian and other necessary

employees.

Section 3. Jurisdiction of District Court

The district court has original jurisdiction in all civil and criminal cases and shall have appellate jurisdiction as prescribed by law.

Section 4. Judicial Districts; District Judges

The number and boundaries of judicial districts shall be established in the manner provided by law but the office of a district judge shall not be abolished during his term. There shall be two or more district judges in each district. Each judge of the district court in any district shall be a resident of that district at the time of his selection and during his continuance in office.

Section 5. Qualifications; Compensation

Judges of the supreme court, the court of appeals and the district court shall be learned in the law. The qualifications of all other judges and judicial officers shall be prescribed by law. The compensation of all judges shall be prescribed by the legislature and shall not be diminished during their term of office.

Section 6. Holding other Office

A judge of the supreme court, the court of appeals or the district court shall not hold any office under the United States except a commission in a reserve component of the military forces of the United States and shall not hold any other office under this state. His term of office shall terminate at the time he files as a candidate for an elective office of the United States or for a nonjudicial office of this state.

Section 7. Term of Office; Election

The term of office of all judges shall be six years and until their successors are qualified. They shall be elected by the voters from the area which they are to serve in the manner provided by law.

Section 8. Vacancy

Whenever there is a vacancy in the office of judge the governor shall appoint in the manner provided by law a qualified person to fill the vacancy until a successor is elected and qualified. The successor shall be elected for a six year term at the next general election occurring more than one year after the appointment.

Section 9. Retirement, Removal and Discipline

The legislature may provide by law for retirement of all judges and for the extension of the term of any judge who becomes eligible for retirement within three years after expiration of the term for which he is selected. The legislature may also provide for the retirement, removal or other discipline of any judge who is disabled, incompetent or guilty of conduct prejudicial to the administration of justice.

Section 10. Retired Judges

As provided by law a retired judge may be assigned to hear and decide any cause over which the court to which he is assigned has jurisdiction.

Section 11. Probate Jurisdiction

Original jurisdiction in law and equity for the administration of the estates of deceased persons and all guardianship and incompetency proceedings, including jurisdiction over the administration of trust estates and for the determination of taxes contingent upon death, shall be provided by law. Section 12. Abolition of probate court; status of judges.If the probate court is abolished by law, judges of that court who are learned in the law shall become judges of the court that assumes jurisdiction of matters described in section 11.

Section 13. District Court Clerks

There shall be in each county one clerk of the district court whose qualifications, duties and compensation shall be prescribed by law. He shall serve at the pleasure of a majority of the judges of the district court in each district.

ARTICLE VII: ELECTIVE FRANCHISE

Section 1. Eligibility; Place of Voting; Ineligible Persons

Every person 18 years of age or more who has been a citizen of the United States for three months and who has resided in the precinct for 30 days next preceding an election shall be entitled to vote in that precinct. The place of voting by one otherwise qualified who has changed his residence within 30 days preceding the election shall be prescribed by law. The following persons shall not be entitled or permitted to vote at any election in this state: A person not meeting the above requirements; a person who has been convicted of treason or felony, unless restored to civil rights; a person under guardianship, or a person who is insane or not mentally competent.

Section 2. Residence

For the purpose of voting no person loses residence solely by reason of his absence while employed in the service of the United States; nor while engaged upon the waters of this state or of the United States; nor while a student in any institution of learning; nor while kept at any almshouse or asylum; nor while confined in any public prison. No soldier, seaman or marine in the army or navy of the United States is a resident of this state solely in consequence of being stationed within the state.

Section 3. Uniform Oath at Elections

The legislature shall provide for a uniform oath or affirmation to be administered at elections and no person shall be compelled to take any other or different form of oath to entitle him to vote.

Section 4. Civil Process Suspended on Election Day

During the day on which an election is held no person shall be arrested by virtue of any civil process.

Section 5. Elections by Ballot

All elections shall be by ballot except for such town officers as may be directed by law to be otherwise chosen.

Section 6. Eligibility to Hold Office

Every person who by the provisions of this article is entitled to vote at any election and is 21 years of age is eligible for any office elective by the people in the district wherein he has resided 30 days previous to the election, except as otherwise provided in this constitution, or the constitution and law of the United States.

Section 7. Official Year of State

The official year for the state of Minnesota commences on the first Monday in January in each year and all terms of office terminate at that time. The general election shall be held on the first Tuesday after the first Monday in November in each even numbered year.

Section 8. Election Returns to Secretary of State; Board of Canvassers

The returns of every election for officeholders elected statewide shall be made to the secretary of state who shall call to his assistance two or more of the judges of the supreme court and two disinterested judges of the district courts. They shall constitute a board of canvassers to canvass the returns and declare the result within three days after the canvass.

Section 9. Campaign Spending Limits

The amount that may be spent by candidates for constitutional and legislative offices to campaign for nomination or election shall be limited by law. The legislature shall provide by law for disclosure of contributions and expenditures made to support or oppose candidates for state elective offices.

ARTICLE VIII: IMPEACHMENT AND REMOVAL FROM OFFICE

Section 1. Impeachment Powers

The house of representatives has the sole power of impeachment through a concurrence of a majority of all its members. All impeachments shall be tried by the senate. When sitting for that purpose, senators shall be upon oath or affirmation to do justice according to law and evidence. No person shall be convicted without the concurrence of two-thirds of the senators present.

Section 2. Officers Subject to Impeachment; Grounds; Judgment

The governor, secretary of state, auditor, attorney general and the judges of the supreme court, court of appeals and district courts may be impeached for corrupt conduct in office or for crimes and misdemeanors; but judgment shall not extend further than to removal from office and disqualification to hold and enjoy any office of honor, trust or profit in this state. The party convicted shall also be subject to indictment, trial, judgment and punishment according to law.

Section 3. Suspension

No officer shall exercise the duties of his office after he has been impeached and before his acquittal.

Section 4. Service of Impeachment Papers

No person shall be tried on impeachment before he has been served with a copy thereof at least 20 days previous to the day set for trial.

Section 5. Removal of Inferior Officers

The legislature of this state may provide for the removal of inferior officers for malfeasance or nonfeasance in the performance of their duties.

Section 6. Recall

A member of the senate or the house of representatives, an executive officer of the state identified in section 1 of article V of the constitution, or a judge of the supreme court, the court of appeals, or a district court is subject to recall from office by the voters. The grounds for recall of a judge shall be established by the supreme court. The grounds for recall of an officer other than a judge are serious malfeasance or nonfeasance during the term of office in the performance of the duties of the office or conviction during the term of office of a serious crime. A petition for recall must set forth the specific conduct that may warrant recall. A petition may not be issued until the supreme court has determined that the facts alleged in the petition are true and are sufficient grounds for issuing a recall petition. A petition must be signed by a number of eligible voters who reside in the district where the officer serves and who number not less than 25 percent of the number of votes cast for the office at the most recent general election. Upon a determination by the secretary of state that a petition has been signed by at least the minimum number of eligible voters, a recall election must be conducted in the manner provided by law. A recall election may not occur less than six months before the end of the officer's term. An officer who is removed from office by a recall election or who resigns from office after a petition for recall issues may not be appointed to fill the vacancy that is created.

ARTICLE IX: AMENDMENTS TO THE CONSTITUTION

Section 1. Amendments; Ratification

A majority of the members elected to each house of the legislature may propose amendments to this constitution. Proposed amendments shall be published with the laws passed at the same session and submitted to the people for their approval or rejection at a general election. If a majority of all the electors voting at the election vote to ratify an amendment, it becomes a part of this constitution. If two or more amendments are submitted at the same time, voters shall vote for or against each separately.

Section 2. Constitutional Convention

Two-thirds of the members elected to each house of the legislature may submit to the electors at the next general election the question of calling a convention to revise this constitution. If a majority of all the electors voting at the election vote for a convention, the legislature at its next session, shall provide by law for calling the convention. The convention shall consist of as many delegates as there are members of the house of representatives. Delegates shall be chosen in the same manner as members of the house of representatives and shall meet within three months after their election. Section 5 of Article IV of the constitution does not apply to election to the convention.

Section 3. Submission to People of Constitution Drafted at Convention

A convention called to revise this constitution shall submit any revision to the people for approval or rejection at the next general election held not less than 90 days after submission of the revision. If three-fifths of all the electors voting on the question vote to ratify the revision, it becomes a new constitution of the state of Minnesota.

ARTICLE X: TAXATION

Section 1. Power of Taxation; Exemptions; Legislative Powers

The power of taxation shall never be surrendered, suspended or contracted away. Taxes shall be uniform upon the same class of subjects and shall be levied and collected for public purposes, but public burying grounds, public school houses, public hospitals, academies, colleges, universities, all seminaries of learning, all churches, church property, houses of worship, institutions of purely public charity, and public property used exclusively for any public purpose, shall be exempt from taxation except as provided in this section. There may be exempted from taxation personal property not exceeding in value $200 for each household, individual or head of a family, and household goods and farm machinery as the legislature determines. The legislature may authorize municipal corporations to levy and collect assessments for local improvements upon property benefited thereby without regard to cash valuation. The legislature by law may define or limit the property exempt under this section other than churches, houses of worship, and property solely used for educational purposes by academies, colleges, universities and seminaries of learning.

Section 2. Forestation

To encourage and promote forestation and reforestation of lands whether owned by private persons or the public, laws may be enacted fixing in advance a definite and limited annual tax on the lands for a term of years and imposing a yield tax on the timber and other forest products at or after the end of the term.

Section 3. Occupation Tax; Ores

Every person engaged in the business of mining or producing iron ore or other ores in this state shall pay to the state an occupation tax on the valuation of all ores mined or produced, which tax shall be in addition to all other taxes provided by law. The tax is due on the first day of May in the calendar year next following the mining or producing. The valuation of ore for the purpose of determining the amount of tax shall be ascertained as provided by law. Funds derived from the tax shall be used as follows: 50 percent to the state general revenue fund, 40 percent for the support of elementary and secondary schools and ten percent for the general support of the university.

Section 4. Motor Fuel Taxation

The state may levy an excise tax upon any means or substance for propelling aircraft or for propelling or operating motor or other vehicles or other equipment used for airport purposes and not used on the public highways of this state.

Section 5. Aircraft

The legislature may tax aircraft using the air space overlying the state on a more onerous basis than other personal property. Any such tax on aircraft shall be in lieu of all other taxes. The legislature may impose the tax on aircraft of companies paying taxes under any gross earnings system of taxation notwithstanding that earnings from the aircraft are included in the earnings on which gross earnings taxes are computed. The law may exempt from taxation aircraft owned by a nonresident of the state temporarily using the air space overlying the state.

Section 6. Taconite Taxation

Laws of Minnesota 1963, Chapter 81, relating to the taxation of taconite and semi-taconite, and facilities for the mining, production and beneficiation thereof shall not be repealed, modified or amended, nor shall any laws in conflict therewith be valid until November 4, 1989. Laws may be enacted fixing or limiting for a period not extending beyond the year 1990, the tax to be imposed on persons engaged in

(1) the mining, production or beneficiation of copper,

(2) the mining, production or beneficiation of copper-nickel, or

(3) the mining, production or beneficiation of nickel. Taxes imposed on the mining or quarrying of taconite or semi-taconite and on the production of iron ore concentrates therefrom, which are in lieu of a tax on real or personal property, shall not be considered to be occupation, royalty, or excise taxes within the meaning of this amendment.

Section 7. Repealed.

Section 8. Parimutuel Betting

The legislature may authorize on-track parimutuel betting on horse racing in a manner prescribed by law.

ARTICLE XI: APPROPRIATIONS AND FINANCES

Section 1. Money Paid from State Treasury

No money shall be paid out of the treasury of this state except in pursuance of an appropriation by law.

Section 2. Credit of the State Limited.

The credit of the state shall not be given or loaned in aid of any individual, association or corporation except as hereinafter provided.

Section 3. Internal Improvements Prohibited; Exceptions

The state shall not be a party in carrying on works of internal improvements except as authorized by this constitution. If grants have been made to the state especially dedicated to specific purposes, the state shall devote the proceeds of the grants to those purposes and may pledge or appropriate the revenues derived from the works in aid of their completion.

Section 4. Power to Contract Public Debt; Public Debt Defined

The state may contract public debts for which its full faith, credit and taxing powers may be pledged at the times and in the manner authorized by law, but only for the purposes and subject to the conditions stated in section 5. Public debt includes any obligation payable directly in whole or in part from a tax of state wide application on any class of property, income, transaction or privilege, but does not include any obligation which is payable from revenues other than taxes.

Section 5. Public Debt and Works of Internal Improvement; Purposes

Public debt may be contracted and works of internal improvements carried on for the following purposes:

(a) to acquire and to better public land and buildings and other public improvements of a capital nature and to provide money to be appropriated or loaned to any agency or political subdivision of the state for such purposes if the law authorizing the debt is adopted by the vote of at least three-fifths of the members of each house of the legislature;

(b) to repel invasion or suppress insurrection;

(c) to borrow temporarily as authorized in section 6;

(d) to refund outstanding bonds of the state or any of its agencies whether or not the full faith and credit of the state has been pledged for the payment of the bonds;

(e) to establish and maintain highways subject to the limitations of article XIV;

(f) to promote forestation and prevent and abate forest fires, including the compulsory clearing and improving of wild lands whether public or private;

(g) to construct, improve and operate airports and other air navigation facilities;

(h) to develop the state's agricultural resources by extending credit on real estate security in the manner and on the terms and conditions prescribed by law;

(i) to improve and rehabilitate railroad rights-of-way and other rail facilities whether public or private, provided that bonds issued and unpaid shall not at any time exceed $200,000,000 par value; and

(j) as otherwise authorized in this constitution.
As authorized by law political subdivisions may engage in the works permitted by (f), (g), and (i) and contract debt therefor.

Section 6. Certificates of Indebtedness

As authorized by law certificates of indebtedness may be issued during a biennium, commencing on July 1 in each odd-numbered year and ending on and including June 30 in the next odd-numbered year, in anticipation of the collection of taxes levied for and other revenues appropriated to any fund of the state for expenditure during that biennium.

No certificates shall be issued in an amount which with interest thereon to maturity, added to the then outstanding certificates against a fund and interest thereon to maturity, will exceed the then unexpended balance of all money which will be credited to that fund during the biennium under existing laws. The maturities of certificates may be extended by refunding to a date not later than December I of the first full calendar year following the biennium in which the certificates were issued. If money on hand in any fund is not sufficient to pay all non-refunding certificates of indebtedness issued on a fund during any biennium and all certificates refunding the same, plus interest thereon, which are outstanding on December 1 immediately following the close of the biennium, the state auditor shall levy upon all taxable property in the state a tax collectible in the ensuing year sufficient to pay the same on or before December 1 of the ensuing year with interest to the date or dates of payment.

Section 7. Bonds

Public debt other than certificates of indebtedness authorized in section 6 shall be evidenced by the issuance of bonds of the state. All bonds issued under the provisions of this section shall mature not more than 20 years from their respective dates of issue and each law authorizing the issuance of bonds shall distinctly specify the purposes thereof and the maximum amount of the proceeds authorized to be expended for each purpose. A separate and special state bond fund shall be maintained on the official books and records. When the full faith and credit of the state has been pledged for the payment of bonds, the state auditor shall levy each year on all taxable property within the state a tax sufficient with the balance then on hand in the fund to pay all principal and interest on bonds issued under this section due and to become due within the ensuing year and to and including July 1 in the second ensuing year. The legislature by law may appropriate funds from any source to the state bond fund. The amount of money actually received and on hand pursuant to appropriations prior to the levy of the tax in any year shall be used to reduce the amount of tax otherwise required to be levied.

Section 8. Permanent School Fund; Source; Investment; Board of Investment

The permanent school fund of the state consists of

(a) the proceeds of lands granted by the United States for the use of schools within each township,

(b) the proceeds derived from swamp lands granted to the state,

(c) all cash and investments credited to the permanent school fund and to the swamp land fund, and

(d) all cash and investments credited to the internal improvement land fund and the lands therein. No portion of these lands shall be sold otherwise than at public sale, and in the manner provided by law. All funds arising from the sale or other disposition of the lands, or income accruing in any way before the sale or disposition thereof, shall be credited to the permanent school fund. Within limitations prescribed by law, the fund shall be invested to secure the maximum return consistent with the maintenance of the perpetuity of the fund. The principal of the permanent school fund shall be perpetual and inviolate forever. This does not prevent the sale of investments at less than the cost to the fund; however, all losses not offset by gains shall be repaid to the fund from the interest and dividends earned thereafter. The net interest and dividends arising from the fund shall be distributed to the different school districts of the state in a manner prescribed by law.
A board of investment consisting of the governor, the state auditor, the secretary of state, and the attorney general is constituted for the purpose of administering and directing

the investment of all state funds. The board shall not permit state funds to be used for the underwriting or direct purchase of municipal securities from the issuer or the issuer's agent.

Section 9. Investment of Permanent University Fund; Restrictions

The permanent university fund of this state may be loaned to or invested in the bonds of any county, school district, city or town of this state and in first mortgage loans secured upon improved and cultivated farm lands of this state, but no such investment or loan shall be made until approved by the board of investment; nor shall a loan or investment be made when the bonds to be issued or purchased would make the entire bonded indebtedness exceed 15 percent of the assessed valuation of the taxable property of the county, school district, city or town issuing the bonds; nor shall any farm loan or investment be made when the investment or loan would exceed 30 percent of the actual cash value of the farm land mortgaged to secure the investment; nor shall investments or loans be made at a lower rate of interest than two percent per annum nor for a shorter period than one year nor for a longer period than 30 years.

Section 10. Exchange of Public Lands; Reservation of Rights

As the legislature may provide, any of the public lands of the state, including lands held in trust for any purpose, may be exchanged for any publicly or privately held lands with the unanimous approval of the governor, the attorney general and the state auditor. Lands so acquired shall be subject to the trust, if any, to which the lands exchanged therefor were subject. The state shall reserve all mineral and water power rights in lands transferred by the state.

Section 11. Timber Lands Set Apart as State Forests; Disposition of Revenue

School and other public lands of the state better adapted for the production of timber than for agriculture may be set apart as state school forests, or other state forests as the legislature may provide. The legislature may also provide for their management on forestry principles. The net revenue therefrom shall be used for the purposes for which the lands were granted to the state.

Section 12. County, Township or Municipal Aid to Railroads Limited

The legislature shall not authorize any county, township or municipal corporation to become indebted to aid in the construction or equipment of railroads to any amount that exceeds five percent of the value of the taxable property within that county, township or municipal corporation. The amount of taxable property shall be determined by the last assessment previous to the incurring of the indebtedness.

Section 13. Safekeeping State Funds; Security; Deposit of Funds; Embezzlement

All officers and other persons charged with the safekeeping of state funds shall be required to give ample security for funds received by them and to keep an accurate entry of each sum received and of each payment and transfer. If any person converts to his own use in any manner or form, or shall loan, with or without interest, or shall deposit in his own name, or otherwise than in the name of the state of Minnesota; or shall deposit in banks or with any person or persons or exchange for other funds or property, any portion of the funds of the state or the school funds aforesaid, except in the manner prescribed by law, every such act shall be and constitute an embezzlement of so much of the aforesaid state and school funds, or either of the same, as shall thus be taken, or loaned, or deposited or exchanged, and shall be a felony. Any failure to pay over, produce or account for the state school funds, or any part of the same entrusted to such officer or persons as by law required on demand, shall be held and be taken to be prima facie evidence of such embezzlement.

Section 14. Environment and Natural Resources Fund

A permanent environment and natural resources trust fund is established in the state treasury. Loans may be made of up to five percent of the principal of the fund for water system improvements as provided by law. The assets of the fund shall be appropriated by law for the public purpose of protection, conservation, preservation, and enhancement of the state's air, water, land, fish, wildlife, and other natural resources. The amount appropriated each year of a biennium, commencing on July 1 in each odd-numbered year and ending on and including June 30 in the next odd-numbered year, may be up to 5-1/2 percent of the market value of the fund on June 30 one year before the start of the biennium. Not less than 40 percent of the net proceeds from any state-operated lottery must be credited to the fund until the year 2025.

Section 15. Outdoor Heritage, Clean Water, Parks and Trails, and Arts and Cultural Heritage; Sales Tax Dedicated Funds

Beginning July 1, 2009, until June 30, 2034, the sales and use tax rate shall be increased by three-eighths of one percent on sales and uses taxable under the general state sales and use tax law. Receipts from the increase, plus penalties and interest and reduced by any refunds, are dedicated, for the benefit of Minnesotans, to the following funds: 33 percent of the receipts shall be deposited in the outdoor heritage fund and may be spent only to restore, protect, and enhance wetlands, prairies, forests, and habitat for fish, game, and wildlife; 33 percent of the receipts shall be deposited in the clean water fund and may be spent only to protect, enhance, and restore water quality in lakes, rivers, and streams and to protect groundwater from degradation, and at least five percent of the clean water fund must be spent only to protect drinking water sources; 14.25 percent of the receipts shall be deposited in the parks and trails fund and may be spent only to support parks and trails of regional or statewide significance; and 19.75 percent shall be deposited in the arts and cultural heritage fund and may be spent only for arts, arts education, and arts access and to preserve Minnesota's history and cultural heritage. An outdoor heritage fund; a parks and trails fund; a clean water fund and a sustainable drinking water account; and an arts and cultural heritage fund are created in the state treasury. The money dedicated under this section shall be appropriated by law. The dedicated money under this section must supplement traditional sources of funding for these purposes and may not be used as a substitute. Land acquired by fee with money deposited in the outdoor heritage fund under this section must be open to the public taking of fish and game during the open season unless otherwise provided by law. If the base of the sales and use tax is changed, the sales and use tax rate in this section may be proportionally adjusted by law to within one-thousandth of one percent in order to provide as close to the same amount of revenue as practicable for each fund as existed before the change to the sales and use tax.

ARTICLE XII: SPECIAL LEGISLATION; LOCAL GOVERNMENT

Section 1. Prohibition of Special Legislation; Particular Subjects

In all cases when a general law can be made applicable, a special law shall not be enacted except as provided in section 2. Whether a general law could have been made applicable in any case shall be judicially determined without regard to any legislative assertion on that subject. The legislature shall pass no local or special law authorizing the laying out, opening, altering, vacating or maintaining of roads, highways, streets or alleys; remitting fines, penalties or forfeitures; changing the names of persons, places, lakes or rivers; authorizing the adoption or legitimation of children; changing the law of descent or succession; conferring rights on minors; declaring any named person of age; giving effect to informal or invalid wills or deeds, or affecting the estates of minors or persons under disability; granting divorces; exempting property from taxation or regulating the rate of interest on money; creating private corporations, or amending, renewing, or extending the charters thereof; granting to any private corporation, association, or individual any special or exclusive privilege, immunity or franchise whatever or authorizing public taxation for a private purpose. The inhibitions of local or special laws in this section shall not prevent the passage of general laws on any of the subjects enumerated.

Section 2. Special Laws; Local Government

Every law which upon its effective date applies to a single local government unit or to a group of such units in a single county or a number of contiguous counties is a special law and shall name the unit or, in the latter case, the counties to which it applies. The legislature may enact special laws relating to local government units, but a special law, unless otherwise provided by general law, shall become effective only after its approval by the affected unit expressed through the voters or the governing body and by such majority as the legislature may direct. Any special law may be modified or superseded by a later home rule charter or amendment applicable to the same local government unit, but this does not prevent the adoption of subsequent laws on the same subject. The legislature may repeal any existing special or local law, but shall not amend, extend or modify any of the same except as provided in this section.

Section 3. Local Government; Legislation Affecting

The legislature may provide by law for the creation, organization, administration, consolidation, division and dissolution of local government units and their functions, for the change of boundaries thereof, for their elective and appointive officers including qualifications for office and for the transfer of county seats. A county boundary may not be changed or county seat transferred until approved in each county affected by a majority of the voters voting on the question.

Section 4. Home Rule Charter

Any local government unit when authorized by law may adopt a home rule charter for its government. A charter shall become effective if approved by such majority of the voters of the local government unit as the legislature prescribes by general law. If a charter provides for the consolidation or separation of a city and a county, in whole or in part, it shall not be effective without approval of the voters both in the city and in the remainder of the county by the majority required by law.

Section 5. Charter Commissions

The legislature shall provide by law for charter commissions. Notwithstanding any other constitutional limitations the legislature may require that commission members be freeholders, provide for their appointment by judges of the district court, and permit any member to hold any other elective or appointive office other than judicial. Home rule charter amendments may be proposed by a charter commission or by a petition of five percent of the voters of the local government unit as determined by law and shall not become effective until approved by the voters by the majority required by law. Amendments may be proposed and adopted in any other manner provided by law. A local government unit may repeal its home rule charter and adopt a statutory form of government or a new charter upon the same majority vote as is required by law for the adoption of a charter in the first instance.

ARTICLE XIII: MISCELLANEOUS SUBJECTS

Section 1. Uniform System of Public Schools

The stability of a republican form of government depending mainly upon the intelligence of the people, it is the duty of the legislature to establish a general and uniform system of public schools. The legislature shall make such provisions by taxation or otherwise as will secure a thorough and efficient system of public schools throughout the state.

Section 2. Prohibition as to Aiding Sectarian School

In no case shall any public money or property be appropriated or used for the support of schools wherein the distinctive doctrines, creeds or tenets of any particular Christian or other religious sect are promulgated or taught.

Section 3. University of Minnesota

All the rights, immunities, franchises and endowments heretofore granted or conferred upon the University of Minnesota are perpetuated unto the university.

Section 4. Lands Taken for Public Way or Use; Compensation; Common Carriers

Land may be taken for public way and for the purpose of granting to any corporation the franchise of way for public use. In all cases, however, a fair and equitable compensation shall be paid for land and for the damages arising from taking it. All corporations which are common carriers enjoying the right of way in pursuance of the provisions of this section shall be bound to carry the mineral, agricultural and other productions of manufacturers on equal and reasonable terms.

Section 5. Lotteries

The legislature shall not authorize any lottery or the sale of lottery tickets, other than authorizing a lottery and sale of lottery tickets for a lottery operated by the state.

Section 6. Prohibition of Combinations to Affect Markets

Any combination of persons either as individuals or as members or officers of any corporation to monopolize markets for food products in this state or to interfere with, or restrict the freedom of markets is a criminal conspiracy and shall be punished as the legislature may provide.

Section 7. No license Required to Peddle

Any person may sell or peddle the products of the farm or garden occupied and cultivated by him without obtaining a license therefor.

Section 8. Veterans Bonus

The state may pay an adjusted compensation to persons who served in the armed forces of the United States during the period of the Vietnam conflict or the Persian Gulf War. Whenever authorized and in the amounts and on the terms fixed by law, the state may expend monies and pledge the public credit to provide money for the purposes of this section. The duration of the Vietnam conflict and the Persian Gulf War may be defined by law.

Section 9. Militia Organization

The legislature shall pass laws necessary for the organization, discipline and service of the militia of the state.

Section 10. Seat of Government

The seat of government of the state is in the city of St. Paul. The legislature may provide by law for a change of the seat of government by a vote of the people, or may locate the same upon the land granted by Congress for a seat of government. If the seat of government is changed, the capitol building and grounds shall be dedicated to an institution for the promotion of science, literature and the arts to be organized by the legislature of the state. The Minnesota Historical Society shall always be a department of this institution.

Section 11. State Seal

A seal of the state shall be kept by the secretary of state and be used by him officially. It shall be called the great seal of the state of Minnesota.

Section 12. Preservation of Hunting and Fishing

Hunting and fishing and the taking of game and fish are a valued part of our heritage that shall be forever preserved for the people and shall be managed by law and regulation for the public good.

ARTICLE XIV: PUBLIC HIGHWAY SYSTEM

Section 1. Authority Of State; Participation Of Political Subdivisions

The state may construct, improve and maintain public highways, may assist political subdivisions in this work and by law may authorize any political subdivision to aid in highway work within its boundaries.

Section 2. Trunk Highway System

There is hereby created a trunk highway system which shall be constructed, improved and maintained as public highways by the state. The highways shall extend as nearly as possible along the routes number 1 through 70 described in the constitutional amendment adopted November 2, 1920, and the routes described in any act of the legislature which has made or hereafter makes a route a part of the trunk highway system.

The legislature may add by law new routes to the trunk highway system. The trunk highway system may not exceed 12,200 miles in extent, except the legislature may add trunk highways in excess of the mileage limitation as necessary or expedient to take advantage of any federal aid made available by the United States to the state of Minnesota.

Any route added by the legislature to the trunk highway system may be relocated or removed from the system as provided by law. The definite location of trunk highways numbered 1 through 70 may be relocated as provided by law but no relocation shall cause a deviation from the starting points or terminals nor cause any deviation from the various villages and cities through which the routes are to pass under the constitutional amendment adopted November 2, 1920. The location of routes may be determined by boards, officers or tribunals in the manner prescribed by law.

Section 3. County State-Aid Highway System

A county state-aid highway system shall be constructed, improved and maintained by the counties as public highways in the manner provided by law. The system shall include streets in municipalities of less than 5,000 population where necessary to provide an integrated and coordinated highway system and may include similar streets in larger municipalities.

Section 4. Municipal State-Aid Street System

A municipal state-aid street system shall be constructed, improved and maintained as public highways by municipalities having a population of 5,000 or more in the manner provided by law.

Section 5. Highway User Tax Distribution Fund

There is hereby created a highway user tax distribution fund to be used solely for highway purposes as specified in this article. The fund consists of the proceeds of any taxes authorized by sections 9 and 10 of this article. The net proceeds of the taxes shall be apportioned: 62 percent to the trunk highway fund; 29 percent to the county state-aid highway fund; nine percent to the municipal state-aid street fund. Five percent of the net proceeds of the highway user tax distribution fund may be set aside and apportioned by law to one or more of the three foregoing funds. The balance of the highway user tax distribution fund shall be transferred to the trunk highway fund, the county state-aid highway fund, and the municipal state-aid street fund in accordance with the percentages set forth in this section. No change in the apportionment of the five percent may be made within six years of the last previous change.

Section 6. Trunk Highway Fund

There is hereby created a trunk highway fund which shall be used solely for the purposes specified in section 2 of this article and the payment of principal and interest of any bonds issued under the authority of section 11 of this article and any bonds issued for trunk highway purposes prior to July 1, 1957. All payments of principal and interest on bonds issued shall be a first charge on money coming into this fund during the year in which the principal or interest is payable.

Section 7. County State-Aid Highway Fund

There is hereby created a county state-aid highway fund. The county state-aid highway fund shall be apportioned among the counties as provided by law. The funds apportioned shall be used by the counties as provided by law for aid in the construction, improvement and maintenance of county state-aid highways. The legislature may authorize the counties by law to use a part of the funds apportioned to them to aid in the construction, improvement and maintenance of other county highways, township roads, municipal streets and any other public highways, including but not limited to trunk highways and municipal state-aid streets within the respective counties.

Section 8. Municipal State-Aid Street Fund

There is hereby created a municipal state-aid street fund to be apportioned as provided by law among municipalities having a population of 5,000 or more. The fund shall be used by municipalities as provided by law for the construction, improvement and maintenance of municipal state-aid streets. The legislature may authorize municipalities to use a part of the fund in the construction, improvement and maintenance of other municipal streets, trunk highways, and county state-aid highways within the counties in which the municipality is located.

Section 9. Taxation of Motor Vehicles

The legislature by law may tax motor vehicles using the public streets and highways on a more onerous basis than other personal property. Any such tax on motor vehicles shall be in lieu of all other taxes thereon, except wheelage taxes imposed by political subdivisions solely for highway purposes. The legislature may impose this tax on motor vehicles of companies paying taxes under the gross earnings system of taxation notwithstanding that earnings from the vehicles may be included in the earnings on which gross earnings taxes are computed. The proceeds of the tax shall be paid into the highway user tax distribution fund. The law may exempt from taxation any motor vehicle owned by a nonresident of the state properly licensed in another state and transiently or temporarily using the streets and highways of the state.

Section 10. Taxation of motor fuel

The legislature may levy an excise tax on any means or substance used for propelling vehicles on the public highways of this state or on the business of selling it. The proceeds of the tax shall be paid into the highway user tax distribution fund.

Section 11. Highway Bonds

The legislature may provide by law for the sale of bonds to carry out the provisions of section 2. The proceeds shall be paid into the trunk highway fund. Any bonds shall mature serially over a term not exceeding 20 years and shall not be sold for less than par and accrued interest. If the trunk highway fund is not adequate to pay principal and interest of these bonds when due, the legislature may levy on all taxable property of the state in an amount sufficient to meet the deficiency or it may appropriate to the fund money in the state treasury not otherwise appropriated.

Section 12. Motor Vehicle Sales Tax Apportionment

Beginning with the fiscal year starting July 1, 2007, 63.75 percent of the revenue from a tax imposed by the state on the sale of a new or used motor vehicle must be apportioned for the transportation purposes described in section 13, then the revenue apportioned for transportation purposes must be increased by ten percent for each subsequent fiscal year through June 30, 2011, and then the revenue must be apportioned 100 percent for transportation purposes after June 30, 2011.

Section 13. Motor Vehicle Sales Tax Allocation

The revenue apportioned in section 12 must be allocated for the following transportation purposes: not more than 60 percent must be deposited in the highway user tax distribution fund, and not less than 40 percent must be deposited in a fund dedicated solely to public transit assistance as defined by law.